When I went to Detroit for the Eyes on the Classics car show this year, I had the unique opportunity of sitting at the same table with Mr. Sergio Pininfarina, his wife Giorgia, and Mr. and Mrs. Charles Jordan.

All through the night at the banquet that followed the awards ceremony at which Mr. Pininfarina received a lifetime achievement award, I was formulating in my mind what would be the best approach to ask Mr. Pininfarina to let me dedicate an issue of ***Rosso Ferrari*** to the story of his prestigious Company's involvement with Ferrari.

We were almost at the dessert when I got the courage to do so. And then it happened: the Ferrari magic again.

Mr. Pininfarina was enthusiastic. He called his daughter, Lorenza, to ask her to coordinate with me in carrying out this project.

Since I was on a roll, I asked Mr. Jordan if he would give us his view of the Pininfarina Ferrari automobiles from the angle of a Ferrari fan and owner who also happens to be Vice President of Design for General Motors.

Well, I got it all, including a rare video of Enzo Ferrari speaking about Pininfarina. More than ever, the red mist works on everyone.

I think that we could have found no better way at ***Rosso Ferrari*** to wish all our readers a happy holiday season.

Before I close, all of us wish a fond farewell and many good wishes to Ing. Piero Fusaro as he returns to the Fiat Group, and we welcome back Dr. Luca Cordero di Montezemolo as Chairman, President, and Chief Executive Officer of Ferrari S.p.A.

Giuseppe Greco
Publisher

President and Chief Executive Officer
Ferrari North America, Inc.

CONTENTS

ROSSO FERRARI/FIVE

WINTER 1991

3 **Inside Rosso Ferrari**
Publisher's Message

8 **Ferrari Forum**
Letters to the Editor

10 **Jordan On Pininfarina**
by George Damon Levy

22 **la galleria Pininfarina**
Artist: Dexter Brown

36 **Pininfarina History**
by Gianni Rogliatti

66 **Sergio Pininfarina:**
An exclusive
Rosso Ferrari Interview
by Gianni Rogliatti

Front Cover: Photograph taken from
Pininfarina video tape

Ferrari®

THE OFFICIAL PUBLICATION OF FERRARI NORTH AMERICA

Giuseppe Greco
PUBLISHER

Ferrari North America, Inc.
250 Sylvan Avenue
Englewood Cliffs, New Jersey 07632

Designed and Published By
Hank Forssberg Inc.
Two University Plaza, Suite 208
Hackensack, New Jersey 07601

Henrik J. Forssberg
EDITOR

Nancy Talarico
CREATIVE DIRECTOR/DESIGNER

For Advertising Information Contact
Eileen Walton

Rosso Ferrari Magazine
Two University Plaza, Suite 208
Hackensack, New Jersey 07601
(201) 488-4800 • Telefax (201) 488-5487

OUR THANKS
TO EVERYONE
WHO CONTRIBUTED
EDITORIAL, GRAPHICS
AND PHOTOGRAPHY
FOR
ROSSO FERRARI/FIVE

SPECIAL THANKS

To Lorenza Pininfarina and Fredi Valentini of the Pininfarina Public Relations Department for making this collectible edition of Rosso Ferrari possible. And, of course, a very special thanks to Ing. Sergio Pininfarina for granting us an exclusive interview, thereby providing Rosso Ferrari readers with the opportunity to enjoy this historical documentary of the greatest coachbuilder in the world.

To Charles M. Jordan for sharing his experience and insights into the genius of Pininfarina.

This issue marks the first anniversary of ***Rosso Ferrari*** magazine.

Over the course of the past 12 months, we have obtained exclusive insights into the Ferrari mystique. Our journey has taken us to the birthplace of Enzo Ferrari, to the homes of Ferrari collectors, and to the Ferrari factory for in-depth reports from Piero Ferrari, Deputy Chairman of the Board, as well as Franco Gozzi, Walter Vignale, and Gianni Rogliatti.

We have worked with some of the top names in automotive publishing, including John Dinkel, Editor-at-Large of ***Road & Track***, David E. Davis, Jr., Editor/Publisher of ***Automobile Magazine***, and Hector Bergandi, noted automotive illustrator.

Rosso Ferrari has delved into the personalities of several of the most famous race car drivers of all time, including Juan Manuel Fangio, Mario Andretti and Phil Hill.

There is not enough space to individually thank each person who has helped make ***Rosso Ferrari*** a success. However, we extend our deep appreciation to everyone who has contributed material or granted us an interview.

We also want to thank our advertisers who have supported ***Rosso Ferrari*** throughout our first year of publication.

We look forward to continuing to bring you the most unusual and fascinating stories related to the Ferrari experience as we enter our second year of publication.

Hank Forssberg
Editor

Design. It can be as traditional as an Andrew Wyeth Americana scene, as wildly geometric as a Picasso, or as strangely surreal as the work of Dali.

While defining their periods, these and countless other artistic treasures also transcend time. They never lose appeal.

The art of Sergio Pininfarina is another classic example of timeless design. His automotive bodies are curvaceous sculptures, each able to stand alone as a visual masterpiece.

We are pleased to dedicate ***Rosso Ferrari***/Five to the extraordinary work of Pininfarina.

Pininfarina has influenced the entire field of automotive design. As with all great artists, Pininfarina's contributions are enduring.

Rosso Ferrari salutes Sergio Pininfarina and the design principles that have revolutionized the visual arts.

Nancy Talarico
Creative Director
Designer

'24 Mouton Rothschild isn't something you forget. We were at Claire's summer place.

Or was it The St. Regis?

AN ITT SHERATON LUXURY HOTEL

FIFTH AVENUE AT 55TH STREET, NEW YORK, N.Y. 10022 • TEL 212.753.4500, TELEX 148368, FAX 212.541.4736

EDITOR'S NOTE

As a service to our readers, we are publishing the following letter concerning a special insurance offer designed exclusively for owners of Ferrari automobiles. While this does not constitute an endorsement on the part of Ferrari North America, Inc. or ***Rosso Ferrari*** *magazine, we feel that this information is worth sharing.*

Insuring the physical damage for high-end specialty cars can be extremely costly and even prohibitive for some owners. The high cost for such insurance, as well as the restrictive coverage available, has caused some owners to risk going without or underinsuring their vehicles. This situation has caused many owners to lock up their thoroughbred motorcars in storage facilities or fireproof garages.

Still others may shy away from purchasing certain vehicles simply because they are too expensive to insure.

In response to this problem, Frank B. Hall & Co. has arranged an Automobile Physical Damage Insurance Program for Ferrari owners that provides both improved coverages and very reasonable premiums.

The program provides comprehensive and collision coverages for any Ferrari, as well as any other vintage, classic or sports/racing vehicles. The policy covers all risk of direct physical damage, including earthquake and flood. This program does not provide liability coverage.

Earlier this year, the program was introduced to the Ferrari Club of America in the San Francisco Bay Area. In just five months, the program has received a very favorable response, with 25% of the local Club membership requesting coverage. This represents over $25 million in vehicles, from a 1963 250 GT California to a 1990 F40.

Some of the features include:

- Comprehensive and collision coverage
- Agreed value
- Deductibles ranging from $1,000 to $2,500 depending on the value of the vehicle, subject to a maximum of $5,000 in the aggregate for any one loss

Certain exclusions apply. In addition, vehicles must be kept in locked/secure premises when at their normal garage location.

Annual premiums are determined as follows:

- Base rate of $0.25 per $100 value for vehicles never driven
- Rates increase based on annual mileage
- No annual maximum mileage limit

The program covers cars that are actually driven as well as those that are for exhibit only or are transported to events. Coverage applies anywhere in the United States and Canada. The program is far less restrictive than those of other carriers writing similar coverage. Premium savings have averaged between 30-80% per vehicle.

There is much interest in keeping this program exclusive to Ferrari owners and their cars. Anyone interested in further information should call (415) 543-9370, ext. 650.

Gregory T. Ohner
Vice President
Frank B. Hall & Co.
San Francisco, CA

Correction— On page 45 of ***Rosso Ferrari***/Four, the caption above the photo of the Ferrari 500 Superfast identified the car as a 250 GT Lusso.

When you drive a Ferrari, you drive one-of-a-kind.
When you wear a Brioni, you wear one-of-a-kind.

A commitment to the finest hand-tailored
men's clothing in the world.

HAND-TAILORED IN ITALY SINCE 1945

ROMA • FIRENZE
NEW YORK
55 East 52nd St.

For the location of an authorized Brioni retailer near you, contact
Brioni 610 Fifth Avenue NY, NY 10020 • (212) 956-4155

JORDAN ON PININFARINA

It's difficult to imagine anyone better qualified to comment on Sergio Pininfarina and his influence upon Ferrari design than Charles M. Jordan.

Jordan has been one of design's leading lights from an early age. At 19, he won the prestigious Fisher Body Craftsman's Guild competition. At 29, he became the youngest man to head General Motors' Cadillac Studio. For the last four-and-a-half years Jordan has been responsible for all GM design activities; it's been his mission to restore the automaker to the position of world design leadership it held during the glory years of Jordan's mentors and predecessors, the late Bill Mitchell and Harley Earl. Already there are signs the goal is being achieved. The new Buick Park Avenue is an unqualified success. The 1992 Cadillac Seville and Eldorado, introduced at recent auto shows, have met with overwhelming critical praise. "This is my favorite car of the show," said Mercedes chief stylist Bruno Sacco of the Seville at its introduction at the annual Detroit gathering.

Andrea Pininfarina, Charles M. Jordan, Sergio Pininfarina and Stan Wilen admiring the Cadillac Allante. Jordan collaborated with Pininfarina on the Cadillac Allante project.

Charles M. Jordan, 1957. The young GM designer at work in the advanced studio.

Jordan and Pininfarina enjoy a close personal and professional relationship.

Jordan also has been a Ferrari enthusiast for more than forty years and has enjoyed a close personal and professional relationship with Sergio Pininfarina for most of them. In Jordan's garage are a Ferrari F40 and a Testarossa. In his office at the Eero Saarinen-designed GM Tech Center in Warren, Michigan are some of the finest examples of a Ferrari model collection that numbers over 2000 and a Ferrari literature collection that dates back, literally, to the beginning. A few years ago Jordan collaborated with Pininfarina

Jordan is an avid Ferrarista.

on the Cadillac Allante project. More recently, Jordan was the master of ceremonies at the annual Eyes on the Classics concours, where he had the privilege of presenting his long-time friend with a lifetime achievement award for design.

We sent former ***AutoWeek*** *editor George Damon Levy to talk to Jordan about Pininfarina, Ferrari, and the role Sergio Pininfarina has played in helping to create and sustain the Ferrari legend.*

Battista Pinin Farina. Founder of the world's most renowned "Carrozzeria."

***O**n Ferrari design:*

When you talk about Ferrari design, you're talking about Pininfarina. In the early days Ferrari used a lot of designers. Good, capable designers, people whose work we all admired. But something was missing. Enzo Ferrari realized it was not enough just for his cars to perform like Ferraris, although obviously that was important, but also that they needed to *look* like Ferraris. They had to have a special look, they had to have a specific Ferrari character and identity. That was the final key to establishing the Ferrari mystique.

So he turned to Pininfarina. In those days it was Pinin Farina — two words — and the man in charge wasn't Sergio, but his father, Battista, the company founder. Battista Pinin Farina was considered the best coachbuilder in Italy, which for all intents and purposes meant that he was the best independent coachbuilder in the world.

Enzo Ferrari and Battista "Pinin" Farina are two key figures in the story of Italian motoring at a time when the motor car was becoming an important industrial phenomenon. Ferrari founded his company in 1929 and Pinin Farina founded the Carrozzeria or coachbuilding industry in 1930. But it was in 1952 that these two great names appeared together on the same car, giving origin to a partnership which has surely produced the finest and most sought-after cars of our time.
—Gianni Rogliatti

And so these two gentlemen agreed to meet, and Sergio accompanied his dad to that fateful meeting with Enzo Ferrari. He was just a kid then, fresh out of college, he'd just gotten married a short time before. So you can imagine his surprise when, on the way home from the meeting, his father turned to him and said, "You will be responsible for the design of the Ferraris."

Sergio has been responsible for the design of virtually every Ferrari since, including many of the race cars — forty years of Ferrari design. Over that period he's helped to establish the Ferrari identity and, more importantly, helped to maintain it.

In fact, that's the thing I admire most about Sergio, not just creating the Ferrari character, but maintaining it so skillfully over so

Father and son. Sergio accompanied his father to many of the early meetings with Mr. Ferrari and was given the responsibility for all Ferrari design.

many years. Every Pininfarina Ferrari *looks* like a Ferrari, whether it's front-engined or mid-engined, whether it was designed last week or back in 1952. Now that might not seem like such a big deal to someone outside the design world, but think about it, no one else has done it. Lamborghini? No. Maserati? No. Bugatti? Close. Porsche? Only because they keep doing the same car over and over again, and excuse my prejudice here for a minute but for sheer visual impact no Porsche has

ever been able to measure up to, say, a 348 or a California Spyder.

It's only when you look back at the entire Ferrari history from the first Pininfarina design, the 212 Inter, to the 250 Testa Rossa, to the SWB, the Lusso, the 275 GTB, the Daytona and the Boxer, right up through the Testarossa, that you really appreciate what Sergio has meant to the Ferrari marque. I can't think of a single relationship in the history of the automobile that's resulted in such a long and consistent heritage of outstanding design.

Sergio Pininfarina worked directly with Mr. Ferrari in the development and production of the many Pininfarina-designed Ferrari cars.

On what distinguishes a Pininfarina design:

Pininfarina doesn't do "flashy" cars. Anyone can do a flashy car. The problem with a flashy design is that the flash wears off. Pininfarina designs are timeless. They endure. They wear well. Every one of the cars I just mentioned looks

And so these two gentlemen agreed to meet, and Sergio accompanied his dad to that fateful meeting with Enzo Ferrari. He was just a kid then, fresh out of college, he'd just gotten married a short time before. So you can imagine his surprise when, on the way home from the meeting, his father turned to him and said, "You will be responsible for the design of the Ferraris."

Sergio has been responsible for the design of virtually every Ferrari since, including many of the race cars — forty years of Ferrari design. Over that period he's helped to establish the Ferrari identity and, more importantly, helped to maintain it.

In fact, that's the thing I admire most about Sergio, not just creating the Ferrari character, but maintaining it so skillfully over so many years. Every Pininfarina Ferrari *looks* like a Ferrari, whether it's front-engined or mid-engined, whether it was designed last week or back in 1952. Now that might not seem like such a big deal to someone outside the design world, but think about it, no one else has done it. Lamborghini? No. Maserati? No. Bugatti? Close. Porsche? Only because they keep doing the same car over and over again, and excuse my prejudice here for a minute but for sheer visual impact no Porsche has

Father and son. Sergio accompanied his father to many of the early meetings with Mr. Ferrari and was given the responsibility for all Ferrari design.

as good today as it did when it was new. Of course, in avoiding flashiness, sometimes a new Pininfarina design won't have the initial impact of some of its rivals, but over time it will prove its value.

The Boxer's a good example. It was introduced at the same time as the Lamborghini Countach and the Lotus Esprit, cars that were considered much more spectacular when they first came out. They featured the "wedge look," which was the fashion of the day.

Well, the wedge look came and went. And as spectacular as those cars were, today they look a little dated. Not bad, mind you, but dated. The Boxer isn't dated-looking. The Boxer is like the rest of the Pininfarina Ferraris. It ages, but it doesn't grow old.

On his favorite Ferrari:

I remember the first time I saw the Lusso. I still love that car. When someone asks me to name my favorite Ferrari, I say, "The Lusso." The Lusso is special. Lean and graceful. It looks agile and alive. It has a feeling of "sporty elegance" that's never quite been equalled.

My first Ferrari was a Lusso. In the late '60s I was in Milan on a business trip and I went and visited the local distributor, a spur-of-the-moment thing. I remember asking the owner if he ever took in used Ferraris, because, you know, who's ever seen a Ferrari used car lot? He said he did. Then I asked if he ever took in any Lussos and he said, "Funny you should ask..."

He had me. I took one look at the car and just about fell over. Wine red, black interior. Beautiful beyond words. One of the great experiences of my life was flying down to Milano with my wife a few months later, firing up the Lusso and driving it up the autostrada to Switzerland and on to Germany. I fell in love with that car. I'm still in love with it. The Lusso is one of the all-time best examples of great Pininfarina design.

Charles M. Jordan with his favorite Ferrari: the Lusso. An outstanding example of great Pininfarina design.

Mr. Jordan has visited the factory many times, most recently to take delivery of his F40.

On meeting Enzo Ferrari:

One day back in the early '60s when I was still a young designer, Sergio arranged for me to visit the Ferrari factory. This was my first visit and I had no expectations of meeting Mr. Ferrari. No one got to see Mr. Ferrari unless his name was Ascari or Tazio Nuvolari. . . .Or so I thought.

At the end of the tour, Mr. Ferrari's assistant, Mr. Gozzi, turned to me very nonchalantly and said, "Would you like to meet Mr. Ferrari?" It was like asking a devout Catholic if he wanted to see the Pope.

We talked about design. Mr. Ferrari had a keen interest in design. He understood design. He *knew* how important it was to the success of his cars. It's no accident that Ferraris have always been as beautiful as they are.

Soon it was nearing noon and Mr. Ferrari invited me to lunch in his private dining room in the Cavallino Restaurant. We ate and we talked some more. But the best part came afterwards. We were walking back to the factory when a couple of the engineers pulled up in a 250 2+2 and asked him if he'd take it for a ride. They'd done some brake work and they wanted him to check it out. He asked me if I wanted to go along.

Now, at the time, remember, Ferrari was in his sixties, but he'd also been a pretty successful racing driver in his younger days, and I can tell you Mr. Ferrari was still an aggressive driver. *Really* aggressive. We went through the city of Maranello in about three seconds flat.

THE BEST OF BRIONI . STEFANO RICCI . ARTIOLI . ZILLI. BATTAGLIA, BEVERLY HILLS

That didn't faze me. I thought, "It's his town. He can probably get away with things like that here."

But the thing I'll never forget as long as I live was driving up in the foothills just outside of town. I remember one curve in particular. Totally blind. A wall of rock on one side, a ten-story cliff on the other. No way to see what's coming toward you. And what does Mr. Ferrari do? He cuts right across the inboard lane like a race driver, with no regard to whether anything's coming from the other direction. Never even lifted.

There will always be Ferrari cars, but there'll never, ever be another Enzo Ferrari.

On Sergio Pininfarina, the man:

If someone were to ask me to name the automobile designer I admire most, without hesitation the answer would be Sergio Pininfarina. Sergio is not only a master designer, but a gentleman. He's not the temperamental artist type, trying to pass off eccentricity for talent. He's soft-spoken. Subtle. Maybe even a little reserved. He doesn't try to knock you over the head with how brilliant he is or how important he is, but he has very clear ideas and he expresses them like no one I've ever seen. He's the kind of guy that if you're around him long enough at a business meeting or a social function you find yourself thinking time and time again, "I wish I'd said that. I wish I'd thought of that." And he can do that in English or Italian.

He's also a terrific leader. He has a way of leading people without making them feel like they're being led. Sergio would be the first guy to tell you that he doesn't design the Ferraris, just like I'd tell you I don't design the Chevies. I *lead* the design of the Chevrolets. He *leads* the design of the Ferraris. He has people who run the studios for him, he's had different "chief designers" over the years, but somehow the personality of Sergio is always clear in the design of the car. The consistency. The honesty. The elegance. The sincerity. His personality and leadership come through.

On Sergio Pininfarina's influence behind the scenes:

Every Ferrari is first and foremost a reflection of Enzo Ferrari himself. There isn't any question about that. But there's a lot of Sergio in there. More, I think, than a lot of people realize.

Take the Dino, for example. At the time, Mr. Ferrari didn't want to do a mid-engine street car, had no intention of doing one. A race car, okay. This was back in the '60s, in the days of the 250 LM — another Pininfarina design — the first mid-engine Ferrari to win Le Mans. But a street car? No way.

Sergio changed his mind. Not by bullying or threatening, because no one could bully or threaten Mr. Ferrari even if they wanted to. But by creating a mid-engine car so beautiful Mr. Ferrari couldn't help but embrace it and call it his own.

The car was the Dino Berlinetta Speciale, the original Dino show car. Beautiful car. Wonderful car. A major turning point in automotive design. Without that car there never would have been a Boxer or a Testarossa or an F40. Pure Sergio.

When someone asks me what Sergio Pininfarina has meant to the success of the Ferrari automobile I think of the Lusso and the Boxer and the 500 Superfast; I think of the Dino and the Daytona and the 308; I think of the 212 Inter, the 375 MM and the 410 Super America and I think you can say it all in a single word: Everything.

Baci To You.
Here's to the man who gives a woman Baci, Italy's most romantic—and most delicious chocolate. With the rich satin of dark bittersweet Perugina chocolate. The creme of chopped hazelnuts and milk chocolate, topped with a whole, fresh hazelnut. She knows, in Italian, Baci means kisses. And she also knows that with kisses, it's best to be generous.
XXXX
From Italy
Baci
PERUGINA
Finest Quality Chocolates - Chocolats Surfins
Perugina Chocolates, 636 Lexington Ave. at 54th St., New York, NY 10022.
And, at other fine stores. Inquiries 201-587-8080. Mail order only 1-800-235-2315.
PERUGINA

la galleria Pininfarina

Rosso Ferrari *is pleased to present on the following pages an inspired interpretation by renowned automotive artist Dexter Brown of some of the more famous examples of Pininfarina-bodied Ferrari cars.*

Thanks to Lorenza Pininfarina, **Rosso Ferrari** *is able to share these never-before published works of art. The originals are on display at the corporate headquarters of Pininfarina in Turin, Italy.*

The drama that symbolizes Ferrari cars designed by Pininfarina is vividly captured in these extraordinary paintings.

Ferrari 250
Testa Rossa
1958

The Testa Rossa, built between 1957 and 1962, is known for its racing history. However, the car was designed in two forms: one for customer use and another model for competition. The 1958 250 Testa Rossa has a pontoon-fendered body.

Ferrari 250 GT
1960

The 250 GT has wrap-around rear windows with roof supports angled towards the rear of the car. Other features include a horizontal body line and a shallow rectangular grille seen on cabriolets.

The centrally positioned engine of the Dino Berlinetta Speciale allowed for more design freedom. Numerous stylistic features, such as the concave rear window and lowered front hood, influenced the design of future sports cars.

Dino 206 GT
1967

The Dino 206 GT was created as a more affordable and smaller GT car to broaden the market for Ferrari. The placement of the spare tire horizontally in front, the twin hatchback doors for the engine and the luggage compartment are among its innovative features.

Dino
Berlinetta
Competizione
1967

The Dino Competizione was an experimental prototype with a revolutionary design. The doors open from the center of the roof and the four headlights are grouped together in pairs. Other features include a folding steering wheel and prominent air vents over the wings and the bonnet.

Ferrari 250 P5
1968

Shown in Geneva in 1968,
the 250 P5 was an exercise in styling.
This prototype car has a futuristic
design that includes sharp lines and
dramatically curved windows
which expose the spare tire and rear
engine components.

Ferrari 365
GTB/4
1968

The 365 GTB/4 Daytona is noted for its classic styling with its long nose and short passenger space. The original headlight configuration, concealed behind a plastic noseband, was amended twice for the American market. The noseband was at first eliminated, leaving the headlights fully exposed. The final design featured the headlights in retractable pods.

Ferrari 512S
1969

The 512S Berlinetta Speciale, derived in part from the Can Am sports cars, has a 5-litre V-12 engine. When first introduced to the public, the design featured long rising rear wings and a sloping windshield that was constructed into a one-piece lift-up canopy.

PF Modulo
1970

The symmetrical Modulo opens from the center outward to allow passengers to enter and exit the vehicle. Its modernistic design elements include circular vents on the rear panel, wheel arches, and the grouping of all controls in a sphere.

Ferrari BB
1971

The avant-garde BB Berlinetta Boxer combines the engine elements of a racer with its horizontal cylinders and the style of a sleek sports car. Prominent in its design is the molded air scoop which serves as a bumper.

Ferrari
Testarossa
1984

Aerodynamics play a large role in the design of the 1984 Testarossa. The big air scoops on the side widen at the back to accommodate the radiators. The Testarossa combines the best in mechanical and stylistic innovations.

The high performance GTO Berlinetta features two turbo superchargers and an aerodynamic design without the use of antilift elements. Though evolved from the sports berlinettas, the GTO uses composite materials for some body parts.

Ferrari Mythos
1989

The Mythos is an aerodynamically advanced prototype. Its directional stability at high speed and low coefficient of resistance result in exceptional road handling. The ergonomic styling of the Mythos allows for optimum passenger comfort.

348 tb
348 tb
348 ts

Ferrari

pininfarina

It is not by chance that the greatest coachbuilder and the greatest manufacturer of high performance cars have joined forces to create some of the world's most outstanding automobiles. Destiny played a role in bringing together these two men who shared a mutual desire to achieve the best.

by GIANNI ROGLIATTI

When Battista Farina, affectionately known as "Pinin," decided to set up shop independently from his brother in the spring of 1930, the Scuderia Ferrari was just a few months old. Because Mr. Ferrari was interested only in racing and Mr. Farina in building special bodies for luxury cars, they did not meet until many years later in that momentous encounter as recalled by Mr. Sergio Pininfarina (see interview on page 66).

We may imagine that the young Pinin was seeking the freedom to pursue the design ideas that his creative genius was envisioning. He was prompted to strike out on his own by a group of wealthy friends and customers, as was reported in a journal of the period.

He aimed high, showing no interest in economy cars. His goal was to create the best that the automobile industry could produce worldwide.

1930 Isotta Fraschini 8 B

1931 Cadillac V16

One of his affluent customers was Count Carlo Felice Trossi, who was among the greatest drivers of the time. For him, Pinin built first a body on a Hispano Suiza chassis and shortly after another on the grand Isotta Fraschini 8 B. On this car are many details that made Pinin Farina cars different, such as the double luggage locker.

1933 Alfa Romeo 8 C 2300
Coupe Victoria

While his cars were already winning prizes in the concours d'elegance in Europe, Pinin Farina was studying developments on American cars. For example, the Cadillac 16 cylinders with body "Torpedobateau" showed an interesting styling device which hid the chassis under the elegant louvered bands. Another very advanced design was that of the Alfa Romeo coupe Victoria of 1936 with the extremely raked windshield.

*1936 Alfa Romeo 6 C 2300 "Pescara"
Coupe Aerodinamico*

As early as 1936 Pinin Farina demonstrated his awareness of the importance of aerodynamics by building several cars with well rounded and smooth shapes, among them the Lancia Aprilia of 1936 (with totally enclosed wheels front and rear) and the Alfa Romeo 6 C 2300 Pescara of the same year. The cabriolets and spyders as exemplified in the

1936 Lancia Astura "Boeia"

1936 Lancia Astura "Boeia"

Lancia Astura of 1936 and the Aprilia of 1939 were extremely elegant, thanks to their low and flowing lines.

At the onset of World War II, his work force of 500 people produced about 800 cars per year, no small feat considering that all were specials and most were different from one another.

1939 Lancia Aprilia Sport Spyder

1946 Cisitalia

But it was after the war that Pinin Farina production actively skyrocketed both in quantity and quality. With the Cisitalia built in 1947, Pinin Farina established the new lines of the modern car. A moving sculpture, this car is permanently exhibited in the Museum of Modern Art in New York City. There were no tasks too difficult for the Turinese artist: be it an American car such as the Nash-Healey, the

big Bentley or the supremely elegant Lancia Aurelia of 1955. The master stroke was always there. The tail fins of the Aurelia that enclose the rear window are an example of Pinin's enduring design, since this device is still applied to the latest Ferrari.

1952 Nash-Healey

1955 Lancia Aurelia B 56
Prototype "Florida"

The year 1952 saw impressive accomplishments. The first Ferrari with a Pinin Farina body was unveiled. It was, as every Ferrari fan knows, a Tipo 212 Inter Cabriolet, delivered to a Swiss customer. This car, give or take a *few details, possesses the form of the modern two seater with front engine and rear wheel drive. If you wanted to go racing instead of just promenading down Hollywood Boulevard, then Ferrari and Pinin Farina had what you needed: the spyders and berlinettas with 12 cylinder engines in any capacity from 3 to 5 liters and enough power to blast everything else out of their way. Those were the cars that won every race, from Le Mans on down the line. These cars proved to be a stroke of those two geniuses: the racing car with a body made by a great designer.*

Meanwhile Pinin Farina's mind was racing ahead of time. He reasoned that because the

1952 Ferrari 212 Inter Cabriolet

1954 Ferrari 375 MM Spyder

automobile was a popular means of transportation, the increase in customers would produce more demand for the special cars or the "fuoriserie" as they are called in Italy. It may sound like a paradox, but the point was to mass produce the "fuoriserie." They began in 1953 by producing and selling the Fiat Coupe TV (Turismo Veloce or fast touring). However, the real start was a year later with the Giulietta Spyder, a car that made this shape of body fashionable. It remained in production until 1965 and sold over 27 thousand copies. In 1955 the Peugeot 403 was also presented, marking the beginning of another long lasting cooperation with a foreign builder.

To keep up with the increasing demands of his ideal of mass producing the specials in series, Pinin Farina had meanwhile decided to improve the facilities by building a new factory, which is the one operating today in Grugliasco where they moved in 1958. They had bought a big lot, so they could later expand and build the full scale wind tunnel, the first in Italy and, at the time, one of the few in Europe.

1961 Ferrari 250 SWB

Meanwhile, what about Ferrari? Having built a good variety of bodies on an assortment of Ferrari chassis, including the 4 cylinder Mondial and Testa Rossa models for competition, Pinin Farina turned his attention to the 250 GT chassis, the one with the classic V12 engine.

The body shapes done in the early period between 1955 and 1960 show a great deal of fantasy as well as craftsmanship. Fenders went from rounded to straight and rear windows were flat or wraparound. The air intake in most cases included the fog lamps.

It is the coupe form first seen in 1958 that delivered the most sophisticated idea of a luxury car. Ferrari has retained this form ever since. The two-places-only turret placed amidship of a long clean body goes with the glorious sound of the V12. As if to confirm that smaller is better, they produced the sporting version of the short wheel base chassis, that, when coupled to an aluminum construction and a somewhat tuned

engine, turned unbeatable. One of the most coveted cars today, the 250 GT Berlinetta, is known everywhere as the SWB.

Back to the "normal" wheelbase (2.60 meters instead of the SWB 2.40) there is also the 250 GT 2+2 and the elegant "Lusso," the last of the front engined 250s.

The front engined GT series would continue, though with engines of increasing capacity. This

1963 Ferrari 250 GT Lusso

was needed to accommodate more and more accessories, such as air conditioning and power assistance, which the less sporting customers were requesting. So the 275 GTB was born, and the series continued up to the 365.

Enzo Ferrari, who often said that "the horses must stay in front of the wagon," was

1964 Ferrari 275 GTB Berlinetta

convinced by the performance of his monopostos that progress demanded the horses be positioned in the back. This posed new styling and practical problems to the coachbuilder, but Pinin Farina was up to the challenge. The first mid-engine Ferrari with a Pinin Farina body was the 250 Le Mans. Derived from the "24 Hours" winning cars, this was also the one built to comply with the new rules about minimum numbers built to be eligible in sports

1963 Ferrari 250 Le Mans

racing. A big fuss ensued when the powers that be in sports refused to homologate the car, and Ferrari even decided not to race under the Italian banner. That was when the monopostos were painted white and blue, the colors of the North American racing team, in the final races of the 1964 season. It is one of the early examples where the racing cars were not painted with the traditional national colors.

1965 Dino Berlinetta Speciale

Except for the first car of the lot, the 250 Le Mans was not a 250 but a 275, with a 3300 cc capacity engine instead of 3000. But beautiful it was and still is.

The way was marked for the central-rear engined car to become a reality also in GT form. In 1965 at the Paris Motor show, Pinin Farina displayed a car of singular beauty: on the racing Dino chassis, with a V6 engine of two

liters, there was a curvaceous body with a very low line and a concave rear glass.

The theme was to be refined in successive models until the Dino 206 GT would emerge and go into production in 1967. The classic nature of this design was adapted for subsequent models up to and including the 328 and, in part, the 288 GTO.

Pinin lived long enough to see that car in Paris. After having received the academic title of architect from the Turin Politec-

1967 Ferrari 206 GT

1966 Alfa Romeo 1600 Spyder

nico (one of the most respected engineering schools in Europe) and the Legion d'Honneur from France's President Charles De Gaulle, Pinin Farina died on April 3, 1966 at seventy-three years of age.

His son Sergio took over as President. That same year the Fiat 124 Spyder and the Alfa Romeo Duetto Spyder went into production confirming the old man's sound vision.

Pinin Farina had one dream that he didn't see come true. He once told this writer that a time would come when a man could buy the car he liked most, by having the best looking carrozzeria fitted with mechanical components of different sources. The shape of the car would be the dominant factor, with the innards provided by Fiat, Alfa, Peugeot, Opel or anybody else. This would call for a degree of standardization that even now can be considered a daring proposition. But that was Pinin Farina. In 1961 by decree of the Italian President the family name was changed from Farina to Pininfarina. It has been this way ever since, to preserve the memory of the unforgettable "Pinin".

1968 BLMC 1100
Berlina Aerodinamica

1968 Ferrari Daytona

1969 Ferrari 512 S

With his son Sergio and his son-in-law Renzo Carli managing the Company, the Ferrari models continued with one success after another. The last of the front engined berlinettas, the 365 GTB/4 made its debut in 1971 and is better known as the Daytona.

In that same year, Pininfarina produced the striking P 5 prototype (followed by the P 6 in the fall) to continue the series of the Ferrari sports racers that had stopped at P 4. In 1969, the 512S, a fantastic shape for the small production racing sports car, made its debut. The Modulo of 1970 was built on the same chassis, but with lines and technicalities that could have come straight from a spaceship.

1970 Modulo

The BB is dated 1971, and again it is a step forward in the styling of a Ferrari. Here for the first time a rear mounted flat twelve engine is used for a sports GT car. So advanced was the concept that it is still unchallenged today.

It is difficult to follow each of the projects that the Pininfarina Company brought to fruition over the years within the context of this article. Suffice it to say that the plant at Grugliasco was expanded in 1970, and the following year a center for automatic calculations was added. In 1972 the wind tunnel became operative, allowing the Pininfarina Company to enter into a new era of sophisticated design. An example was the CR 25, an experimental model for a practical car with the then unheard of aerodynamic co-

1971 Ferrari BB

1980 Ferrari Pinin Berlina Prototype

efficient of 0.25. The chassis was Ferrari based.

Later on, in 1978 a shape for a car body was designed with aerodynamic coefficient of only 0.172, at a time when the average for passenger cars was 0.46.

In 1980 the highlight of the 50th Anniversary of the Company was the Pinin Model, a prototype for a four door Ferrari. This car was an example of the maximum capabilities in design and manufacture; a peculiar point was that it had the flat 12 engine front mounted.

1990 Chronos

1982 Pininfarina Spydereuropa

1986 Ferrari GTO Berlinetta

But let's not forget the other cars, like the Beta Montecarlo, or the Quartz prototype on an Audi chassis, or the Samba Cabriolet on a Talbot chassis.

The latter was one of the first products of a new facility, the Pininfarina Studi e Ricerche in Cambiano near Turin, where the prototypes can be designed and built in the utmost secrecy.

The more recent successes of the Pininfarina-designed Ferraris are on the road: the GTO of 1984 and in the same year the Testarossa, a nearly impossible accomplishment even for a big manufacturer.

1986 Ferrari Testarossa

1987 Alfa Romeo 164

1990 Alfa Romeo Spyder

1958 Lancia Florida II

The F40 was released in 1987 and the 348 in 1989, the same year the Mythos prototype was shown.

There are many other cars that should not be forgotten in this condensed history. The Florida II on Lancia chassis, an extremely elegant coupe that was the personal car of Pinin for many years, had a clever hidden rear door to allow an easy access to the rear seats. We cannot forget the Jaguar XJS Special or the 504 Peugeot Cabriolet (this one again produced in series) or the majestic Rolls Royce Camargue Coupe.

1987 Ferrari F40

1989 Mythos

1989 Ferrari 348 ts/tb

1978 Jaguar XJS

1969 Peugeot 504 Cabriolet

Time has passed. Sergio Pininfarina has since taken part in politics, having been elected twice to the European Parliament (in 1979 and again in 1984). In 1983 he was also elected "Honorary Royal Designer for Industry" by the British Royal Society of Arts, an honor bestowed upon his father Pinin 30 years earlier.

The Ferrari 412, last of a series of 2+2 models, was presented in 1985. In 1986 the Cadillac Allante was born. GM's first project with an outside body supplier, the Allante was designed by Pininfarina, built in a brand new factory at San Giorgio, and air shipped to Detroit for completion.

In 1990 there was much to celebrate: 60 years of Company life and a fantastic Ferrari show in Florence "L'Idea Ferrari" where

1975 Rolls Royce Camargue

1986 Cadillac Allante

the strong connection between Ferrari and Pininfarina was clearly illustrated by the drawings and full scale models of many cars.

Perhaps the most interesting feature of this Company is its human side. Sergio Pininfarina's two sons, Andrea and Paolo, and daughter Lorenza are all with him in the Company. Andrea is the General Manager of Industrie Pininfarina, the Company Group operating in the engineering and production field, and Managing Director of Pininfarina Deutschland GmbH and Pininfarina fur Auto-Modell Forschung und Entwicklung GmbH. Paolo is President and Managing Director of Pininfarina Extra, a Company founded in 1988 promoting the Pininfarina trademark and image in all the industrial design areas, except means of transport. Lorenza is taking care, with unequalled grace, of the public relations.

Because his children are involved in so many aspects of the Company's management, Sergio can dedicate part of his time to the Presidency of the Italian Industrialists, a very delicate job to which he was unanimously elected by his fellows.

The Pininfarina family:
Sergio with his lovely wife Giorgia, sons Paolo (far left) and Andrea (far right) and daughter Lorenza.

Gianni Rogliatti was granted the following interview by Sergio Pininfarina exclusively for ***Rosso Ferrari.***

GR Mr. Pininfarina, there is a sort of mystery about the first meeting between your father and Mr. Ferrari. How did it really go?

SP *Mr. Ferrari and my father both had strong personalities. I believe that both wished to establish a business relationship, but, being both very proud men, neither of them wanted to take the first step or ask for a meeting at the other's factory. So it was up to me and some friends to arrange for a meeting to be held on neutral ground.*

GR How did you solve this problem?

SP *We found a small restaurant, halfway between Modena and Turin, and an appointment was made to meet there.*

GR Was it easy for the two men to get along well?

SP *To arrange the meeting had been difficult, but their conversation was easy, spontaneous, and constructive.*

The result of that first meeting was the decision to form an industrial cooperation that started at first with the cabriolet on the 212 chassis that was completed in the spring of 1952. Other models followed rapidly, and so the ball started to roll.

GR What was your personal role at that historic meeting?

SP *I only listened, full of respect.*

But on the way back to Turin, my father decided that everything at Pininfarina related to the new Ferrari program—design, engineering, production, etc—had to be under my direct responsibility.

To me, young engineer, sports car and racing fan, this was a dream come true. I felt like I just had touched the sky with my fingers. Today still, everytime a new Ferrari is born, I feel the same emotion!

Mr. Ferrari, at the beginning, was a bit disappointed and did not expect to discuss such important matters with a young man (I was 25 then, just out of the Turin Polytechnic).

But my commitment and determination were so total that, after a few months, he was happy to deal with a new generation of Pininfarina and granted me his consideration, and then his confidence.

When my father died, Enzo Ferrari showed great confidence that I was worthy to continue my father's work and further develop the company.

I remember at the funeral he told me, "Call me Enzo." Psychologically, this helped me a lot, and also in the following years, he gave me his suggestions and advice as a true second father.

GR How was the design process in those early days?

SP *When a new car had to be done, Ferrari would call us to Maranello for a briefing and to see the mechanical components. Then he would describe how he envisioned the new car. He always thought that a new* *car had to have something special. He had performance in mind, but he wanted beauty, too, as well as functionality, light weight and design personality.*

These were the main objectives that he would give us, the same for all his projects, as they were part of his beliefs and his culture.

GR Was Mr. Ferrari an easy client to please?

SP *Not at all! First of all, he was very impatient. From the start of the project and until the car was completed, he would keep us under constant pressure.*

He would count months, sometimes even days, and not the years that are needed in today's product planning.

Especially in those first years, he would often find our projects not spectacular or impressive enough.

As the years went by, he changed his mind to the point that he wrote in one of his books, "When one sees a Pininfarina car, at the moment one doesn't find anything particularly new or exciting. But those cars, even after 20 years, are still beautiful and actual, while the others have dropped out of fashion."

I believe that no one could get a compliment more positive than this, and I am very proud of it.

GR What would happen, then, if he was not satisfied?

SP *I must say that did not happen often, and, as the time went by our understanding grew, it happened progressively less and less. But when he did not like something, he was frank, sometimes even brutal with his criticism, although always constructive.*

Of course he was exacting, as he wanted to achieve with his cars higher technical objectives than anybody else. I must also say that, even if the mechanics were his specialty, his opinions on design were extremely precious, as he had an uncanny capacity to guess the tastes of the particular clientele to whom his cars were destined.

It is unquestionable that he was satisfied with our work, as, in only a few years, we became the sole designer and builder of Ferrari bodies.

GR What were the problems that you had to solve for Ferrari?

SP *To design a Ferrari body is the university of design and construction.*

One must solve the most difficult problems caused by the very high performance of the Ferrari cars, and, furthermore, with a very limited production.

It was a great school, since to solve a problem for a Ferrari meant to have found a perfect solution for all the other cars. One only has to think of problems such as to maintain the windshield wiper in contact with the windshield at high speeds, or to the "ballooning" of a convertible roof, or to the wind noise.

A car, during the construction phase, would change often. New problems would crop up. Sometimes it was the wheelbase or the tire dimensions that would change, or the volume of the air intakes, that was always not enough.

For us, all these changes were a nightmare. Between Ferrari and us there was an eternal conflict. We wanted low profile front section, and Ferrari, for technical reasons, would do very high water radiators.

My father had taught us the philosophy of the low front section, as it was aerodynamically better, and it would allow a better visibility. And this was in contrast to Ferrari's needs.

If I look back to the cars of the '50s and '60s, I see in a lot of them additional air intakes for the front hood, protections for the carburetors' air intakes, large dimensions flared wheelarch.

In one of those cars, since it was no longer possible to change the shape of the body, we had to add an air intake on the rear mudguards, whose only function was to allow the movement of the rear wheels.

GR It could be said, then, that some design solutions are due to a stroke of genius forced by necessity.

SP *More than strokes of genius, these solutions were inspired by necessity. On the other hand, I am convinced that necessity and difficulties have the positive effect of pushing towards new solutions.*

GR Have you ever proposed a new car model to Mr. Ferrari he had not thought about first?

SP *Yes, there was such an event that has touched me directly. Ferrari was loyal to the front-engine-rear-traction solution for all his cars destined for his customers. This forced the designer to design a higher body to allow space for the exhaust tube under the pavement. On top of that, I had the usual problem of the water radiator.*

Our competitors, on the other hand, had already begun to build central-engined automobiles, and I was insisting to Mr. Ferrari that he should do the same.

I had learned from my father that sports cars had to have a low center of gravity. My Ferraris were about 11 inches higher than their competitors, which had a more modern layout.

For me it was like waging a war using the army and navy, but no air force! I was bound to lose.

Then, at last, Ferrari made up his mind to try the new design, not on one of his cars, but on a Dino, an innovative car that he had conceived in his son's memory.

Naturally, cars with a central engine posed some problems, too: rear visibility, heat dispersion, sound proofing.

We solved all these problems brilliantly on our Dino that we showed in Paris in 1965. Since then, these solutions have influenced the design of the Pininfarina—Ferrari sports cars . . . and of the others.

My father, who in 1965 was very ill, came to the Paris Motor Show for a few hours, saw our Dino and said to everybody, "This is my granddaughter, because my sons made her."

GR Why do you like the Dino best?

SP *Because it was an ideal achievement based on my feelings for the sports cars of the future.*

From that first prototype, a second and third were derived, those with the new powertrain that had the V6 engine placed transversally on the chassis. We built the Dino Berlinetta and the Spyder with the hardtop. From that design, the new Ferraris with the transversally mounted V8 evolved: the large family of the 308, the 208, the 328, and the 208 turbo.

GR There is an ideal line that goes through the design of all your Ferraris over the years. Can you explain how this line of thought ties the front-engined cars of yesterday to the rear-engined cars of today and perhaps to the new generation of front-engined cars of tomorrow? (We hear rumors that there will be new front-engined models again.)

SP *Today's technologies change at an impressive pace. New materials allow the creation of forms that were unthinkable only a few years ago.*

But the philosophy, the concept that remains at the source of the Pininfarina—Ferrari automobiles, is still the same that Mr. Ferrari and my father taught us and that has been responsible for their extraordinary success.

Our clients buy the new models and preserve the old ones with love.

That happens because they perceive clearly that all Ferraris always strive to reach for technical and aesthetic ideals, respecting the functional principles that they have to meet.

With this point in mind, the position of the engine and the type of traction are not all important. They play a secondary role to the "Ferrari Idea" that about one year ago was honored in Florence with a great exhibition where, I can say with pride, the fundamental contribution of Pininfarina was highly visible.

Dino
berlinetta speciale

970

"Why do you like the Dino best?"

"Because it was an ideal achievement based on my feelings for the sports cars of the future."

La Dino 206 GT telaio n. 00114, vettura personale di Sergio Pininfarina